Kackling Kamala's Komikal Kronikle

50 Kamala-isms for the 21st Century

Assembled by Michael Robert Krikorian

Disclaimer
(Don't confuse it with Datclaimer.)

The following pages are a fictional account of things that could well have been said by a presidential candidate. We must look beyond what is to see what was. We cannot be burdened by what was by letting it interfere with what is.

Everything within these pages is fictional reality. It is all based on an all too true story which makes it science fiction.

Any resemblance the thoughts shared within these pages have to things said by someone living or dead or considered possibly dead from the neck up is merely coincidental and only applicable should someone wish to apply them aptly.

It is meant for entertainment purposes only.

Dedication

This book is dedicated to ridiculousness and stupidity without which this offering could not have been completed.

There is no better place to start than at the end. You have to know where you're going if you hope to one day get there.

A note from the ~~Arthur~~ Author

We live in a world that is changing every day. Each day is a new day and is different from the day before. There is no telling what tomorrow will bring because each day brings about new things. But the one thing that remains steadfast is the fact that just when you think you've seen or met the biggest moron in the history of the world, someone will invariably top their efforts!

In a nutshell, that is what this book is all about. It is a guide to help those with functioning brain matter endure what will surely be a future filled with ridiculous nonsequiturs, farcical irreverence and preposterous irrelevance. We're not sure what any of that means, but it sounds really intellectual. That's what matters. In the world of today, it's not what you say but what people think you've said. When they are afraid to admit they don't understand you, then you have reached a point of complete, monopolistic control.

Confusion and chaos are at the heart of the world of political correctness. That is what seems to be the centerpiece of the absurdities. However, most people do not know what absurdities I am talking about. The reason? They choose to be unknowing because ignorance is bliss. They choose not to know what absurdities means.

And so, as we reach the first quarter of the 21st Century, the intelligence bar has been lowered to a point where stupidity can masquerade as intellectual prowess. As a result of political correctness, we are all not allowed to tell someone he's a bloody idiot even if he is a bloody idiot. We must find nicer ways to say the obvious. And yet, how many ways are there to call an idiot an idiot?

Following the lead of the media and certain political candidates for public office, the Institute for

Male Enlightenment and Sensitivity Inclusive Studies has offered up some extremely brilliant thoughts that surely will be espoused by the num nuts who call themselves politicians. It is scary to think people actually think the way our illiterate staff thinks. But they do. And they are following the lead of one particularly incredibly inept "leader" whom we have focused on as the foundation for this literary masterpiece. Now for those of you who don't know, a masterpiece is not a very sexy woman. It is a work of art even if it isn't done by anyone named Art.

Rather than run on and on like the sorts who run for office saying a lot but saying nothing, we will allow the words within this offering to speak for themselves. They are taken directly from the cadence and speech patterns of the inanest drone the political world has ever seen. If she has not already thought to say these things, after reading this book, she most likely will. We hope so. It would mean a lovely plagiarism lawsuit which could net tens of dollars.

With all of that in mind, we hope you will be enlightened by the intellectuals who claim to be democracy's ally when in reality they are democracies adversary.

Kackling Kamala's Komikal Kronikle

It isn't the one who knows something that has to tell you something. It's the one who doesn't know anything that needs to show you that he doesn't know anything by trying to show you he knows something.

Part 1

Geography

When you aren't sure where you are going, you need to realize where you've been and then work backwards.

<u>1</u>

<u>Earth</u>

Earth is this place. It is heated by the sun. The sun is very hot. Earth has this place on it called the United States. It is on a continent called North America. North America is north of South America. It's one of the continents, too. There are several and some start with an A like North America. There are some that don't start with an A. There are other places on other continents that start with many different letters, too. It's the reason we have an alphabet. Those other places have people living there. There are a lot of people living in places who don't live in the United States.

<u>2</u>

<u>Europe</u>

Europe is not something a cowboy uses to tie up a horse. Isn't that interesting? It is a place with a lot of people. Not as many people live there as live in other places. But more people want to live there than they want to live in other places. They do so because they have good food. Spaghetti is from Europe. So is pizza. You really have to try pizza sometime. You get the best pizza at a pizza restaurant. It has tomato sauce and cheese.

<u>3</u>

<u>Euthanasia</u>

The young people of the world are important. We need to learn more about them in order to better understand them. Euthanasia is important, but no more important than those on other continents like Mexico and Hawaii. None of them should be neglected or ignored. Youths are the future whether or not they live in Asia.

4

Countries

The difference between countries is that they are different countries. Each is different because they're different. Different is not bad. It's just different. To know the difference is to recognize that there is a difference. This is what makes the world different.

5

Austria

Austria is a country and a continent, too! Isn't that amazing? The people in Austria love kangaroos and little bears. They speak English, but it doesn't sound like English spoken by people in other countries that speak English.

<u>6</u>

<u>Antarctica</u>

Unlike some people may believe, Antarctica is not married to Uncle Arctica. Isn't that surprising? It's actually the name of a place with a lot of penguins. They made the movie *March of the Penguins* there. There were a lot of penguins in the movie. Why they chose March rather than April or May is hard to understand. If you look at a map of the world, you will see Antarctica colored white at the bottom of the map, unless you turn the map over. Then it will be on the top but it will still be white.

7

Rome

Romanian is a term for someone who lives in the city of Rome. People who don't live in Rome are excited to go to other cities, like Rome. They go there to see the pyramids. There is a pyramid in San Francisco, too. A pyramid is a building that is not square. It is exciting to see pyramids.

8

Madagascar

Madagascar is not good. Hate of any kind should never be tolerated. This hate is warranted, however, because it is caused by fossil fueled automobiles. They pollute the earth and cause global warming. That is surely why people are so mad at gas cars.

<u>9</u>

<u>England</u>

England is a place in the country of Europe. England is famous for people speaking English. The country was named after the English language. It is important for people to know that England is where English people live. But there are other people who live in England and other countries, too. However, they are not all English. Only those who live in England are English unless they live in other countries and are English.

<u>10</u>

<u>Finland</u>

Finland is not an amusement park like Sea World even though it may sound like it is. Finland is a country far away from the United States. You can't walk to Finland from the United States. You must take an airplane because it is too far away.

Part 2

Education

Ignorance is a choice not an affliction.

1

School

School is important because you learn important things in school. You cannot learn important things without going to school and learning the important things they teach in school. There is no limit on important things, and you can learn them in school. There are only so many ditch-digging jobs, and those that there are should be given to illegal aliens who come here to make sure that there is work for them.

<u>2</u>

<u>Diversity</u>

Diversity means identifying people by their identity. It is good to identify people. People are all diverse. To see the diversity is to identify it. Diversity helps to give identity to people who want to be identified as people. The world needs to be more conscious of diversity in order to be diverse. Without diversity, the world will become less diverse.

<u>3</u>

<u>Economics</u>

Here is a simple explanation of economics. If you have 4 dollars and something costs 6 dollars, you can get it for 17 dollars. The government does that all of the time. It's called economic growth. When you pay 17 dollars for something that only costs 6 and you have only 4 dollars in your pocket, you put more money into circulation because you are paying 17 dollars for something that costs 6 dollars and you only have 4 dollars. That makes everyone happier.

<u>4</u>

<u>Things</u>

When you have something in your hand, you need to decide what you have in your hand. The reason is because what you have in your hand may not be what you have in your hand. The world is filled with things that seem like other things which in turn appear to be different things. You must strive to see what you have in your hand and understand why it's in your hand because your hand holding it. Don't ever think you have something in your hand until you know you have something in your hand.

<u>5</u>

<u>Colors</u>

When the sky is blue, do you ever ask yourself why the sky is blue? Does it matter? When the sky is blue it is only because it is not another color. The same with the ocean. It has color but water does not. Water is clear. Unless it's polluted by capitalist pigs. Then it has colors that are not good unless the polluters support the right things. Then it's polluted by Russia.

<u>6</u>

<u>Computers</u>

Computers are really, really smart. They are smarter than people. They can do a lot of things people can't do. Everything we do is easier because of computers. Think about shopping. Could you buy so much stuff you don't need if you didn't have a computer? And buying stuff is what matters. The more stuff you buy, the more stuff you have. Stuff and computers. That's what we need more of. That's why we have inequity in this world. Equity is not equal. It's having stuff!

7

<u>Cards</u>

You have a deck of cards. There are the 68 cards in the deck. Do you really have a deck of cards? That's what you need to ask yourself. For everything is what you believe it is. That deck of cards could be a dozen eggs if you believe it is. That is freedom.

8

Math

Math is a thing you can learn in school. You can use it to figure out the answer to math problems. If you need to know the answer to a math problem, you need to use math. Everyone needs math. Math is one of the three Rs in education which are reading, writing and math.

<u>9</u>

<u>People</u>

Imagine a world filled with people. People are important to the world. We are all people, and we fill the world. Isn't that exciting? And so, as people who fill the world, we need to make sure we fill our world with people.

<u>10</u>

<u>World War 2</u>

World War 2 was this thing. Something happened in Europe and something happened in Japan. People fought a war they called World War 2. But there were places where no one was fighting. So it wasn't really a world war. It was only the capitalist pigs fighting for their capitalism against some guy with a silly mustache who wanted socialism. A lot like the United States... Except for the guy with the mustache.

Part 3

Death and Taxes

What you see is not always what is. You can only see what your eyes allow you to see.

1

Breathing

What we are is what we can be if we are not what we are. Being is about breathing. If you breathe, you are being. So by all means breathe as often as possible because you have to breathe or you won't breathe. The future depends upon you breathing. But don't breathe too much because there is only so much air. If people breathe too much, we won't be able to breathe because there won't be any air.

2

<u>Climate</u>

The climate is changing. It changes four times every year. Just the other day, it rained. And the day before that, it didn't rain. We must be prepared to take the necessary steps to prevent the climate from changing. We must understand that the future of the planet depends upon rain, and sometimes we don't get enough. That is called drought. Repeat after me. Drought. Now drought is one of those words like through and though. It has the "ough" sound but doesn't sound like rough.

<u>3</u>

<u>Dying</u>

Dying is not a good thing. We must fight against dying. If you die, you are no longer alive. This is not okay. For there is what is, and there is what can be. If you die, you no longer can be. And more importantly, you can't pay taxes.

4

Murder

Murder is what happens when one person kills another person. Murder can be a good thing because it reduces the rate of attempted murder. But it doesn't have to be one person killing another person. Did you see Jaws? The shark killed people. Sharks kill a lot of people and eat them. Kind of like a Thanksgiving party at Jeffery Dahmer's house. Parties are fun! People should have more parties and have as many people as possible for dinner.

<u>5</u>

<u>Drugs</u>

We have all the right people working on the drug problem. That is the key to our success. We have a crack staff and a joint committee. Who is better to deal with drugs than those who understand drugs. Drug users understand drugs are drugs. There are drugs for those who use drugs no matter if they use them or they don't use them. We must not interfere in the work of those who work.

6

Poker

Poker is a game played with cards. You try to match the cards and make sets. If you win, you yell, "Gin". I guess you do that because you are ordering a drink.

Poker is easy to learn, but you should never play for money. If you do, you could lose money. Money is needed by everyone to pay taxes. If you pay taxes, the government can continue to send the money to foreign countries to protect their borders. Borders are important to other countries. We want to help them keep their borders secure.

7

Houses

Houses are an example of unfairness. Some people don't have houses. They are called homeless. They don't work. They do all of the things everyone else who owns a house does but they don't have houses. And you know houses have bathrooms, too. Isn't that amazing? When people came to this country, there were no houses. There were no bathrooms either because there were no houses. People obviously didn't need them. We need to make this country what it once was. A giant homeless encampment so everyone is truly equal.

8

The Moon

The moon is this round thing in the sky that gives off light at night. It also has something to do with climate change just like everything else in the world. The moon has something to do with the oceans. There isn't an ocean on the moon. But that doesn't matter. We have a lot of oceans here.

<u>9</u>

<u>Science</u>

Science is very scientific. Science is what scientists do because they are scientific. Science changes constantly. It is whatever scientists say it is because they understand science and they are scientific. Scientists are very smart because they understand science is science. We need more scientists so that we can understand science.

10

Why

When you don't know why, then you need to ask why if you want to know why. Things don't have to be understood to be understood. Why is a question word like what and who. If it comes at the beginning of a sentence, it means the sentence will end with one of those squiggly things called a question mark. Repeat that. Question Mark. Now there is no such thing as an answer mark, but there should be. However, you should never forget that many sentences end with parole.

Part 4

General Knowledge
Major Concern

Everything you know is known by someone else. The question is what do you know and why do you know it?

1

The Ocean

The ocean is filled with water. Water is good. We need water. Everybody should drink water. Fish need water. And without fish, we wouldn't have fish restaurants. In San Francisco, there are a lot of fish restaurants. They serve fish at the fish restaurants.

2

<u>Cars</u>

Cars are vehicles that move. They have four wheels. They are driven by people. They have a motor that is responsible for all of the pollution in the world that is causing the planet to become hotter. The planet is hotter. We know that because it is. That's because that's what people who make money telling us it's getting hotter tell us.

3

Clothes

Clothes are things you wear. It doesn't matter if you wear pants or skirts. What matters is that you are allowed to wear clothes. If you buy them, make sure they fit or they won't fit. It's not easy to find pants that fit. But there is more to clothes than just clothes. You have to wash your clothes or they will be dirty all the time. Don't you just hate that? You can often have a stain where it looks like you peed on yourself. That isn't a good thing even if you pee on yourself. But it's best not to pee on yourself.

4

<u>Baseball</u>

Baseball is a game with bases and balls. They both start with the same letter. B! When you play baseball, you run from one base to another if you get a chance to run from one base to another. If you don't, then you don't get to run from one base to another. It all depends upon the ball. If someone catches the ball, then you are not allowed to run to the base. It's really a fun game!

<u>5</u>

<u>Truth</u>

The truth is something you can't make up because it's true. True means something is true. It's important to tell the truth whenever you can so long as it is something you want to tell someone. If it isn't, then you shouldn't tell the truth because telling the truth might mean having to tell someone something you don't want to tell them.

<u>6</u>

52

<u>Rights</u>

We all have rights. We also have lefts. If we didn't, then we wouldn't know if it's right or left because we don't have lefts or rights. Rights are things you can do like breathing and blinking. If you're not sure what lefts are, don't worry. Just remember it is your right to do lefts. So if you know what lefts are, you are free to do them because that is your right.

7

Democracy

Democracy is something you don't understand because you think you do. We all need democracy. It has nothing to do with freedom but it is freedom. You can't have freedom without democracy. The Democrat Party is named after freedom. Freedom is doing what the Democrat Party tells you to do. You are always free to do as the Democrat Party says you can do. It's really that simple!

<u>8</u>

<u>Telephones</u>

A telephone is a thing you can talk on. You can talk to another person on a telephone who isn't even in the same place. You can say something to them. And then they say something back to you on the telephone. It really is amazing! It's like having a conversation.

<u>9</u>

<u>Oil</u>

Oil comes from dinosaurs that are no longer alive. If they were, they would be very scary because they are big! We should all be glad there are no more dinosaurs. But if there were, they would make oil which is a bad thing. Oil is what is needed to make gasoline for cars.

10

Goldilocks

Goldilocks is a person who identifies as a girl. As such, her pronouns are her and she. She could identify as a boy if she chose to do that. Then her pronouns would be he and him. But she has more than one other choice. She could be any of 100 different identifiers.

Goldilocks lived in Wyoming because there are forests in Wyoming. Bears live in forests. She had a run in with some bears. Her story is titled *Goldilocks and the Three Bears*. So maybe there were five or six bears. No one knows why her parents named her Goldilocks. Seems like a ridiculous name. She must have been born during the Summer of Love. People gave their children all kinds of names then. You should read the story so maybe you will know why her parents named her Goldilocks.

Part 5

Meet and Potatoheads

No one really knows anything, but everyone knows something.

1

Hollywood

Hollywood is a place where people make moving pictures. Moving pictures is short for movies. Can you say moving pictures? Try it. Say it with me. Moving pictures. They make pictures move in Hollywood by taking a lot of little pictures and putting them in order. When they do, the people in the pictures actually move. It's so incredible! But they have to be careful to make sure the pictures are in the right order. The person who does that is called the person who puts the pictures in the right order.

2

Meat

Meat comes from animals. Some people eat meat. Some don't. Vegetarians are not doctors who treat animals. They are people who don't eat meat. They eat only vegetables. Vegetables are renewable resources like dirt clods. There are animals who eat meat. They are called meat eaters. We are animals, and most of us are meat eaters. But some are not. Veterinarians are doctors for dogs, cats, horses, ostriches, skunks and animals other than humans. Not all veterinarians are vegetarians. Some are meat eaters.

<u>3</u>

<u>Housing</u>

A house is a place where people live. It doesn't have to be more than one people. One people is called a person. Now that person could be alone in the house or he, she, it, they, that, them, could live with other people. That would be his, her, its, their, family. But not necessarily. The other people might be friends if they have friends. A friend is someone who you know. Or maybe not. It all depends upon who you call a friend. Maybe the other people could be renting rooms from the capitalist pig who owns the house. They are just people who don't own a house themselves.

The President of the United States lives in a house. It is a white house. It is big. It has many rooms. Some of them have names like bedroom and office.

<u>4</u>

<u>Traveling</u>

Traveling abroad is different from traveling as a broad. A person who cross-dresses travels as a broad. However, such terminology can be a source of confusion for many. We must refrain from using such derogatory terms. So rather than saying you are traveling as a broad, it's better to say you are a broad traveling. But either way, it's offensive because it's nobody's business if you are home or away.

<u>5</u>

<u>Asphalt</u>

Asphalt is not a medical condition like hemorrhoids and constipation. It is a type of pavement for streets like concrete. Isn't that exciting? It is black in color which makes it different from concrete which is white. However, it is black because it uses oil. So concrete is better because it is made without oil.

<u>6</u>

<u>Borders</u>

Borders can be a problem. Especially if they are bored. They don't always leave when you ask them to leave and then you have to evict them. But you shouldn't because then they would be homeless. But there are times when you can't be nice to someone who is overstaying his welcome. But borders should always be secure. They should have the only key to their door so they are safe. Our borders are secure.

7

Labels

Labels are important. We all have labels, and we need to continually call attention to our label. If we don't, then we are no better than places that don't call attention to labels. Do you want to live in a country that doesn't have labels for everyone? How would you know what color someone is if you don't have labels identifying them? You can't just look at someone and see he is black or white, can you? Labels make sure we keep everyone separated and divided. That is a good thing. If people are separated and divided, they can't unite against those who are separated and divided.

8

<u>Voting</u>

Democracy is counting every vote that counts. We must count every vote that counts but not those that don't count. We can't trust the voters because they vote. We can't trust them to vote right. Only the votes we believe are right count and should be counted. That's why everyone should vote early and often to make sure their vote is counted each time.

<u>9</u>

<u>Television</u>

Television was invented by someone. Radio was, too. Both televisions and radios are in most homes. People can listen to the radio and watch television. It's really exciting! They can see people doing things on television. On radio they can only listen to people doing things.

<u>10</u>

<u>A.I.</u>

Artificial intelligence is artificial, and it's intelligent. Intelligent means smart. Smart is good. We should all be smart. If we embrace artificial intelligence, we will embrace something smart. That makes us smart.

Artificial Intelligence is short for AI. AI is sort of like IT except it is different. A and I are vowels. I and T are a vowel and a consonant. Did you know that? There are five of vowels. A-E-I-O-U, and sometimes Y like in the word why. Isn't that incredible?

Other Titles You Might Enjoy...
(If you're a masochist)

Picking Your Knows
101 Famous Sayings
(No one ever said)

A Stereotype Is Not Sony
102 More Famous Sayings

I Will Retire When I Get A Flat
103 More Famous Sayings

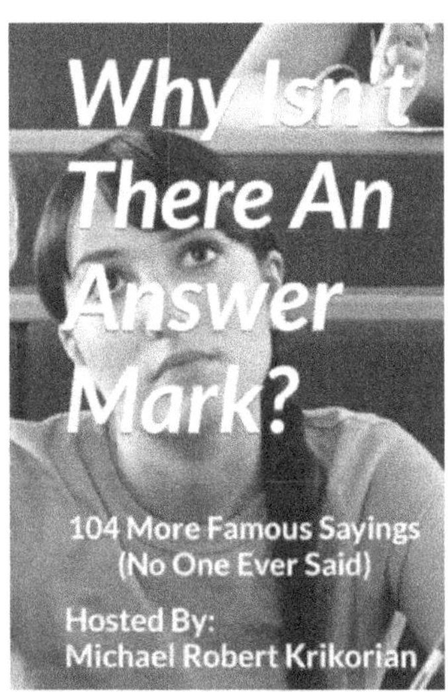

Why Isn't There An Answer Mark?
104 More Famous Sayings

Goldilocks And The Three Bears
The Autobiography of Goldie Locks

God's Not Politically Correct
He's Just Correct

**Technology Is Not God's Ally
It's His Adversary**

**2099
Part 1
The Glaxine Chip**

**2099
Part 2
The Race To Escape Freedom**

**2099
Part 3
Solution, Revolution or Execution**

Kackling Kamala's Komikal Kronikle

The Male Sensitivity Tests

The Umpire's Sensitivity Test

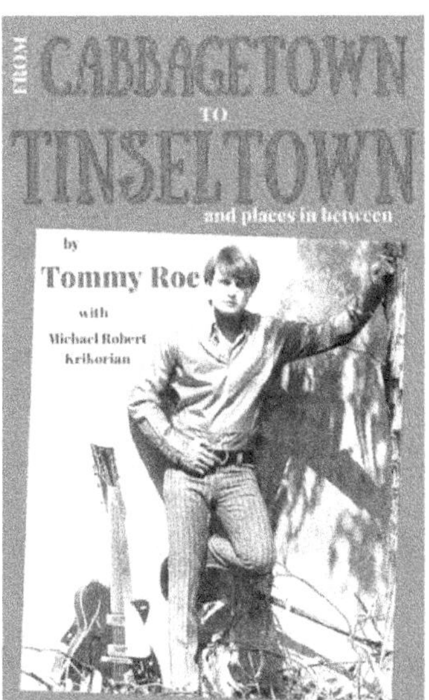

**From Cabbagetown to Tinseltown
and places in between
The Autobiography of Tommy Roe**

**And Speaking of Scorpions...
The Autobiography of Herman Rarebell**

About the Author

Michael Robert Krikorian is an acclaimed author of over 30 books on a variety of subjects and topics. His works range from autobiographies to books on Christian Faith and those meant for laughs. His hope is that his work brings a smile to those in need of laughter.

www.ingramcontent.com/pod-product-compliance
Lightning Source LLC
Chambersburg PA
CBHW051649250726
48653CB00007B/2569